W9-BXW-933

CRAFTS
OF THE ANCIENT WORLD

THE CRAFTS AND CULTURE OF
THE ANCIENT EGYPTIANS

Joann Jovinelly and Jason Netelkos

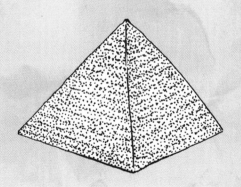

the rosen publishing group's
rosen
central

WITHDRAWN
WINCHESTER PUBLIC LIBRARY
WINCHESTER, MA 01890

To Angela, my goddess of grace

Published in 2002 by The Rosen Publishing Group, Inc.
29 East 21st Street, New York, NY 10010

Copyright © 2002 by The Rosen Publishing Group, Inc.

First Edition

All rights reserved. No part of this book may be reproduced in any form without permission in writing from the publisher, except by a reviewer.

Library of Congress Cataloging-in-Publication Data

Jovinelly, Joann.
The crafts and culture of the ancient Egyptians / Joann Jovinelly and Jason Netelkos.
p. cm. — (Crafts of the ancient world)
Includes bibliographical references and index.
Summary: Describes easy-to-make crafts that replicate the arts of ancient Egypt. Includes historical material, a timeline, a glossary, and resources.
ISBN 0-8239-3509-4 (library binding)
1. Egypt—Civilization—To 332 B.C.—Juvenile literature. 2. Creative activities and seat work—Juvenile literature. [1. Handicraft—Egypt. 2. Egypt—Civilization—To 332 B.C.] I. Title. II. Series.
DT61 .J68 2002
932'.01—dc21

2001004140

Manufactured in the United States of America

Note to Parents
Some of these projects require tools or materials that can be dangerous if used improperly. Adult supervision will be necessary when projects require the use of a craft knife, an oven, a stovetop, plaster of paris, or pins and needles. Before starting any of the projects in this book, you may want to cover your work area with newspaper or plastic. In addition, we recommend using a piece of thick cardboard to protect surfaces while cutting with craft or mat knives. Parents, we encourage you to discuss safety with your children and note in advance which projects may require your supervision.

CONTENTS

THE CULTURE

THE CRAFTS

Before the Egyptians harnessed the waters of the Nile River, taking advantage of its regular flooding to irrigate their farmlands, earlier settlements formed there, farther from its banks, on higher ground. From 5000 BC, Egypt's earliest settlers came to what was then a lush green land from surrounding areas such as Palestine and Syria. Much later, around 3000 BC, people from Iraq sailed up the Nile River to trade with the Egyptians. Some remained, attracted by its fertile farmlands, and began to build mud huts and grow crops.

Most of what is associated with Egyptian culture, such as strong religious beliefs and artistic skills, dates from the time of the pharaohs, or kings, (2686–1085 BC). This time is known as the Dynastic Period and is divided into sections called the Old, Middle, and New Kingdoms. This is the rich, creative period that will be covered in this book.

Egyptians relied on the Nile for food, water, and commerce.

More than anything else, the geography of Egypt and its mighty Nile River helped to shape its civilization for thousands of years. The Nile kept the lands around it well irrigated, and the Egyptians discovered many useful methods to harness its power and harvest its resources. The silt, or mud, along its banks was used to form the earliest mud brick shelters, its waters provided abundant fish and papyrus plants, and the river itself carried travelers and merchandise to many points throughout Egypt. The river also kept the Egyptians safe from invasion. Its northern territory was sheltered by the Delta—a marshy coastline far too shallow for boats. The southern lands were bordered by cataracts—hazardous water rapids that also made traveling risky. The length of the Nile in between these two points, however—the area that served the Egyptians for centuries—was calm and predictable. The Nile protected Egypt

The dark, snaking line on this map of ancient Egypt represents the Nile River, which sustained and protected Egyption civilization.

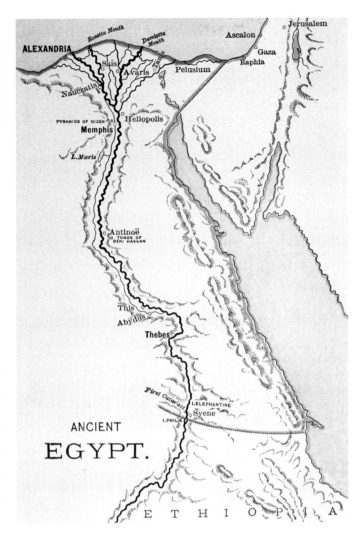

from harm and fed its people, supporting millions of lives.

Before pharaohs ruled Egypt (between 5500 and 3100 BC), its people created the first irrigation system by carving out sections of earth around the riverbanks of the Nile. These sections, or reservoirs, trapped water when the Nile overflowed. The water was then channeled to agricultural areas farther inland, greening desert lands. This new system of irrigation greatly increased Egypt's farmland, and it enabled farmers to plant several crops each year, such as wheat, flax (a plant from which linen is made), green vegetables, and fruits. Agricultural labor became more organized and cooperative, with people working in teams to farm the land. As a result, fewer Egyptians starved, and the population began to grow. Because food was no longer scarce and survival no longer so difficult, some Egyptians were able to turn their attention to other pursuits, such as art.

Another important change occurred at this time that would be critical for the growth of Egypt's culture. Egyptians used to live within a loose collection of small villages and tribes. The population began to swell, thanks to irrigation and improved agriculture. Land disputes began to develop, so its territory was divided into two halves, Upper and Lower Egypt. Later, around 3100 BC, all of Egypt would be united, worship the same gods, share the same beliefs, and coexist peacefully under the rule of one pharaoh. At this point, Egypt became the world's first nation. This was the beginning of the Old Kingdom (2575–2150 BC), considered by most to be Egypt's greatest age, and a period of its history that it would try to recreate during the Middle (2040–1640 BC) and New Kingdoms (1540–1070 BC). These

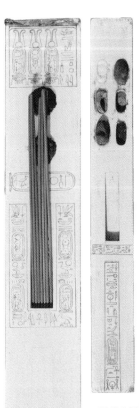

This ancient Egyptian scribe's palette contains reed pens and wells for red and black ink.

two later periods saw significant changes in climate that had a profound impact on Egyptian culture, beliefs, and systems of government.

DAILY LIFE

Egypt was a class-based society, which means its people were divided by the type of work that they did and how wealthy they were. The royal family—the family of the pharaoh—lived in structures that historians now believe were small villas made of wood and mud brick. Inside were private areas for worship, small pools of water filled with fish and plants, and fine furniture and decorations. The mostly male nobility (members of the ruling class) who surrounded the royal family lived in similar structures and had abundant food and leisure time. The nobles were referred to as "servants of the gods" and were revered by society. Architects, mathematicians, astronomers, doctors, and druggists were usually included in the noble class.

Egyptian physicians and druggists, in fact, were among the most skilled in the ancient world. Doctors performed simple surgery and recorded medical information in scrolls—the first surviving medical books. Pharmacists had recipes for preparing drugs, and there is evidence that the Egyptians used opium to control pain, as well as many other remedies created from herbs and plants.

Unlike children of today, most young Egyptians never learned to read or write. Only a few specially chosen boys, most of them from upper-class families, attended school, where they would be taught reading, writing, and arithmetic. Classes continued for about ten years before each boy was required to learn a specific trade or profession; for instance, boys could choose to be doctors, priests, or, in most circumstances, scribes. The profession of scribe (writer of official documents) was considered an advanced trade, and those with this title often performed tasks for the royal family, including recreating damaged documents, collecting taxes, and keeping official records.

Other respected trades included carpentry, metalworking, jewelry making, weaving, and sculpting. Those who did these jobs, though highly regarded, were considered middle class. These individuals worked long hours and lived in the poorer sections of Egypt, crowded into small villages.

The lowest social class was made up mainly of slaves. Slaves lived in the most crowded sections of Egypt, closest to Memphis, the capital of Egypt during the Old Kingdom. The homes of slaves were usually two-story buildings made entirely of mud brick. They were simple and had few furnishings other than a sitting stool and a primitive bed for sleeping. Small windows near the ceiling allowed fresh air to circulate. Most families stored grain on their property and kept small farm animals, such as chickens. The women of the house stayed at home, baked bread, dried fruit, and made the family's clothing. The men worked every day from dawn until dusk doing various jobs, most of which required hard, exhausting labor.

While it has long been thought that slaves were entirely responsible for the building of Egypt's pyramids, most historians now believe that members of every class took part in their construction in some manner, each person working in the service of the pharaoh for whom the tomb was being created. Farmers would have provided a large part of that labor, too, especially during the months in which the Nile River overflowed and working the land was impossible.

This bas-relief shows two sculptors chiseling a statue. Egyptian slaves were often the most productive artisans in the ancient world.

BELIEFS

The Egyptians had a strong religious faith that enriched every part of their lives. They considered their pharaoh to be godlike, but they also worshiped as many as 2,000 other gods. Some of the most famous gods were Osiris, Isis, Horus, Hathor, Anubis, and Thoth. Historians and archaeologists agree that the existence of these many gods has its origin in the scattered villages of the early, not yet unified Egypt. Each village

The Egyptians were among the first people to depict both religious subjects and scenes from daily life. In this image, Ra, the hawk-headed sun god, stands in the solar boat next to the sacred ibis.

Ra was the chief god of the Egyptians throughout the Dynastic Period. They believed that he was born with the dawn every morning and that he died an elderly man at each sunset. When the sky darkened at night, the Egyptians believed that Ra traveled to the underworld, or Duat, the same place where they believed the dead resided.

Another important Egyptian belief was the idea that the dead would live again if certain rituals were followed. To the Egyptians, the underworld was a place in which the dead were judged. To escape safely from Duat, and judgment, to the afterworld, Egyptians felt that they needed many material items and provisions, such as food and drink, personal goods, and important writings that took the form of hieroglyphs (characters that represented words and sounds). These writings, which were found near the mummified bodies of pharaohs, are now known as the Book of the Dead. They contained all the magical information that a pharaoh would need to pass through the dangers of Duat to heaven, which Egyptians called the Field of Reeds. One section of the Book of the Dead describes a final test that takes place in the Hall of Two Truths. This test had to be passed in order

worshiped its own god, and after the unification of the nation, these gods were adopted and worshiped by all Egyptians. Yet, throughout the Dynastic Period, each of the nation's forty-two districts, or nomes, continued to have its own god. The most important of these gods was named Ra, the hawk-headed sun god. Ra took on many different forms at different times of the day; for instance, at dawn Ra was thought to take on the appearance of a scarab beetle called Khepri. Ra would be worshiped in these various forms throughout the day.

to successfully reach the Field of Reeds. It was here that Anubis, the god of the dead, weighed the dead person's heart to see if it was "heavy with sin." To the Egyptians, this represented a judgment about a person's behavior during his or her life.

Because the pharaohs were important royalty who governed Egypt through the centuries, their burials often took place in elaborate stone tombs, several of which still exist today. The most famous group of tombs is found west of the Nile River and by modern-day Cairo, outside of the ancient city of Memphis, in a cluster known as the Great Pyramids of Giza. Another group of tombs, the Valley of the Kings, rests farther from the Nile in a drier, more barren section of Egypt.

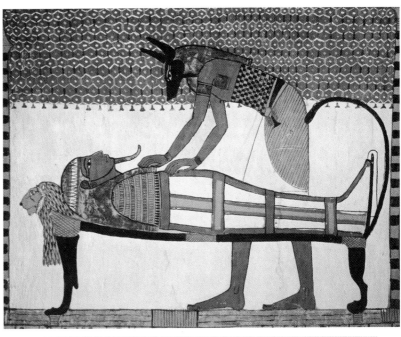

This is a Nineteenth Dynasty painting of the jackal-headed god Anubis preparing the body of Sennedjem, a prominent tomb workman, for entombment.

WARFARE

Ancient Egypt was one of the most enduring civilizations in history partly because it was very rarely gripped by war. As we have already seen, its geography discouraged invasions by enemies. It also discouraged Egyptian acts of aggression against neighboring lands. Because the Nile provided ample amounts of food and other resources (except during periods of drought or famine), Egyptians did not need to look beyond their borders for sustenance. In addition, Egyptians feared dying outside of their homeland; they dreaded the thought of being buried in a foreign place, without the customary funeral rites being performed.

A crude army was formed in the time of the Old Kingdom, the same core military force that grew to protect Egypt during its height of military skill hundreds of years later during the New Kingdom. This force usually fought using only hand-to-hand combat and without any carefully planned strategy.

Throughout the Dynastic Period, even with an organized, united force serving under the absolute rule of one pharaoh, the Egyptian army fell many times to occupiers from surrounding areas, including Ethiopia, Persia, Greece, and Rome. In times of peace, the army also helped move the large stone blocks used to construct the pyramids, which still stand today.

LANGUAGE

The ancient Egyptians developed a complex system of writing known as hieroglyph. Hieroglyphs are symbols and pictures that represent sounds, words, and letters. All together, more than 6,000 different symbols have been identified. The Egyptians used these symbols for everything from keeping daily records and writing medical texts to posting signs in temples and inscribing magical spells on the interior walls of royal tombs.

Since the last known hieroglyph was inscribed—in approximately AD 394—archaeologists and historians alike have tried to decode this ancient and beautiful system of symbols. For centuries, people had discovered remnants of the symbols but could not decipher their meanings. It was not until a 1799 expedition to Egypt by Napoleon Bonaparte and a group of distinguished French scholars that the mystery of the hieroglyphs was finally revealed. The greatest discovery for the group, and for the world, was a block of stone that would later be named for the city of Rosetta, where it was found.

The Rosetta Stone was a crucial discovery because it contained three separate versions of the same text, each written in a different language. The first version is written in demotic, an ancient Egyptian language that predates the hieroglyphs. The second is written in Greek, an ancient language that is still in use today. The third version is written in hieroglyphs.

After years of studying the Rosetta Stone, which dates to the year 196 BC, scholars finally cracked its code by using the Greek text to help translate the hieroglyphs. The meaning of each hieroglyph could be discovered once it was compared to its Greek equivalent. Jean-Francois Champollion was credited with its final translation in 1822. After this breakthrough, scholars from all over the world could read the ancient writings of the Egyptians, confirming or disproving many previous assumptions about the civilization.

ART

Egyptian civilization is best known for its stunning achievements in the arts. While much of the Egyptian art we see in museums today was crafted for the tombs of the royal pharaohs, most ancient Egyptians enjoyed some art in their daily lives, mostly in the form of face painting and jewelry. Both men and women used eye paint and other cosmetics, which were made from natural minerals that were ground on small palettes. In addition, the interior walls of many Egyptian homes were decorated with some of the earliest examples of fresco painting.

Historians believe that Egyptian craftsmen often worked together, sharing workshops in the major cities of the day, such as Memphis. It was also common for temples to have their own team of craftsmen on site, as did two of the most important Egyptian temples that have been discovered, Luxor and Karnak. These groups of craftsmen produced some of the most exquisite artifacts of the ancient world, commonly colored with warm earth tones and gleaming metals, such as gold. Pottery was also quite common, and the Egyptians used clay for making vases, vessels, figurines, and even coffins. Toward the end of the Dynastic Period, Egyptians' portraits were often painted

The Rosetta Stone featured one text inscribed in three different languages. It enabled scholars to translate, decode, and understand hieroglyphs.

and attached to their coffins. Archaeologists believe these funerary paintings date from a period when Rome invaded Egypt and began to influence its artistic traditions.

The Age of the Pyramids

When you think of ancient Egypt, the first image that probably comes to mind is the majestic pyramids, known the world over for the feat of engineering and construction that they represent. These awesome structures, several rising as much as 500 feet above a desert foundation, are situated along the Nile River. The three main pyramids were built during the Old Kingdom (the Age of Pyramids) for the pharaohs Menkaura, Khafra, and Khufu. Three smaller constructions near them were probably "queen's" pyramids, designed to house the mummified remains of the wives and children of the pharaohs. These were not the first pyramids that were built, however.

King Djoser ordered Imhotep, a scholar, to build his tomb, the first step pyramid (so called because it rises in levels) during the Third Dynasty, around 2630 BC, several hundred years before the Menkaura, Khafra, and Khufu pyramids were built. The steps of Djoser's

The cut stone bricks that were assembled to form the great pyramids are visible in this photo of the pyramid of Khufu. The pyramid of Khafra rises in the background.

pyramid were called *mastabas* and were slabs of mud brick, the same material that comprised most of Egypt's ancient constructions. The later pyramids were made entirely of stone after the four-sided pyramid design was perfected.

The later pyramids were massive constructions, built entirely of cut stone blocks—each weighing an estimated 5,000 pounds! They were transported along the Nile River and carried up a series of ramps to their final destination. Scientists now estimate that each pyramid took the labor of 100,000 men over a twenty-year period to assemble all the stones necessary for its construction.

While the exteriors of the pyramids are plain and simple, hidden inside them is a complicated, mazelike system of tunnels and secret rooms. Some of the tunnels lead to chambers that served as the dead pharaoh's tomb and were crowded with treasure. Other tunnels and rooms may have been built to confuse those who would attempt to rob the pyramid of its riches. Through the centuries, nearly every sacred tomb was raided of its valuables. The most notable tomb, discovered in 1922, was that of the boy pharaoh Tutankhamen. His chamber was filled with hundreds of artifacts, untouched since they were placed there some 3,000 years earlier. Many of these artifacts traveled the world on exhibition but have since returned to permanent display at the Egyptian Museum of Cairo.

A visitor crouches as he explores the mazelike interior of the Great Pyramid of Cheops. Tombs, some crowded with treasures and personal belongings, were often joined by narrow tunnels like this one.

A camel and rider approach the pyramids of Giza. The Great Pyramids are considered one of the greatest wonders of the ancient world.

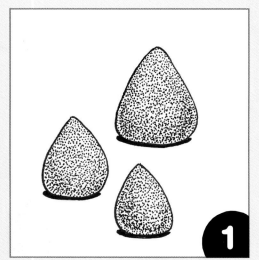

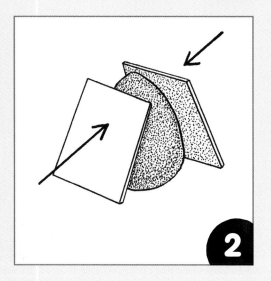

Egyptian Pyramids*

Recreate one of the wonders of the world by constructing small models of the Egyptian pyramids of Giza.

* ADULT SUPERVISION IS REQUIRED FOR THIS CRAFT.

YOU WILL NEED
- **Sand clay (see recipe below)**
- **Cardboard**
- **Ruler**

Sand Clay Recipe
3 cups sand (beach or play sand)
1 1/2 cups cornstarch
3 teaspoons of powdered alum
2 1/2 cups of hot tap water

Combine all dry ingredients in a large saucepan. Add the water and cook over low heat. Stir constantly for about five minutes, or until the mixture becomes thick and heavy. Remove from the stovetop and scoop the clay onto a cookie sheet to cool before modeling.

Step 1
Separate your sand clay into three parts: half for the large pyramid, and the second half in two equal portions for the two smaller pyramids. Form each lump of clay into a rounded ball shape. Begin with the smaller balls first. Form each ball into the shape of a chocolate "kiss."

Step 2
Using two pieces of cardboard of equal size, apply even and gentle pressure to opposite sides of the clay "kiss." Apply the same equal pressure on the remaining two sides of your pyramid. Then repeat, working opposite sides alternately, until all four sides are the same and are slanted to a single point, just like a pyramid.

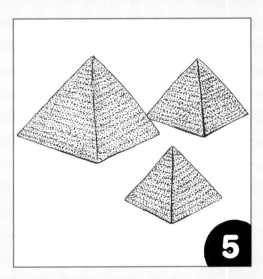

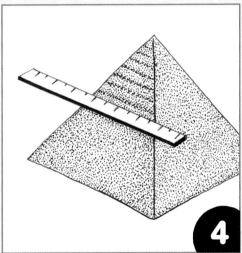

Step 3
Examine your pyramid shape from a standing position. Continue shaping it if you are not satisfied with the four-sided shape. With your fingers, dab a little tap water to the angles to smooth any bumps in the clay.

Step 4
Once you have your desired shape, gently tap each side of the pyramid repeatedly with the straight edge of a ruler. This will provide the simulated texture of stone blocks.

Step 5
Repeat this same process for each pyramid, allowing each to dry for two to three days, and rotating if necessary. After the third day, place the pyramids on their sides to allow the bottoms to dry.

Writing and Literature

Scribes were highly regarded for their ability to read and write hieroglyphs, as well as the earlier Egyptian languages, and their services were sought after throughout the centuries. These educated men had much greater responsibilities than mere record-keeping, however. For example, they were responsible for inscribing temples and pharaohs' tombs. Scribes earned considerable respect from all people and were never expected to engage in manual labor. They were also looked to for advice and were expected to behave morally, setting a good example and establishing professional standards for future generations of scribes.

The rules for writing hieroglyphs were complicated, and interpreting the symbols was difficult. Scribes often worked long hours, inscribing monuments, temples, tombs, papyri (an early form of paper made from the papyrus plant), and even scarabs (ancient stamps in the shape of a dung beetle). Some scarabs were used as seals on letters and official documents and included basic information about the pharaohs, such as their names and the years they served Egypt. Other scarab stamps were more elaborate, relating the famous incidents that occurred during a pharaoh's reign. Scarabs were also used as sacred amulets and placed over the hearts of the deceased.

Scribes were highly regarded in ancient Egyptian society, not only for their writing abilities, but also for their moral authority.

Scarabs were sometimes made from a popular Egyptian material called faience. Much different from what modern craftspeople refer to when speaking of faience (clay covered with tin enamel), the ancient version was glazed granite (a soda-lime silica glaze was applied to the hardened granite and then the object was fired, or baked, in a hot oven). The results were richly colored and lustrous, and fairly inexpensive. Faience was a simple substitute for the precious stones Egyptians adored but that were in short supply, such as malachite and lapis lazuli. It was easy to carve with hieroglyphs and was used by all classes in Egypt to make beads, jewelry, cooking vessels, statuettes, tiles, and scarabs.

This is a scarab, the dung beetle whose likeness was often used by Egyptians on official seals and protective amulets. Egyptians believed that a giant scarab rolled the sun across the sky each day between dawn and dusk.

The reverse sides of the scarab amulets were inscribed with magical spells. It was a widely accepted Egyptian belief that a scarab worn by the deceased would ease his or her journey to the afterlife. Placed near or on the body of a mummy, along with coffin texts (to ensure the successful passage of the deceased to the next world), these scarabs were also marked with the owner's name. The owner's name, the coffin texts, and the magic spells all had to be written by scribes.

Scarab amulets, like those shown here, were inscribed with names, important events, and other information to commemorate pharaohs and other royalty.

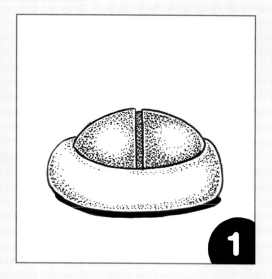

Egyptian Scarab

Make a scarab and inscribe it with ancient magical hieroglyphs just like the Egyptians' sacred amulets.

YOU WILL NEED
- Modeling clay
- Egg-shaped object
- Plaster of paris
- Plastic bag
- Toothpick
- Craft paint

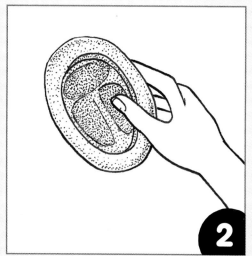

Step 1
Knead a palm-sized portion of your modeling clay, and shape it into an oval. Imprint its center with an egg-shaped or oval object (such as a plastic egg), or use your fingers. This will be your scarab mold. If you want to make several scarabs, you will need a mold for each.

Step 2
Make the design of your scarab by marking the oval (the beetle's body) with three thumb imprints. One horizontal thumb imprint becomes the scarab's head, and two vertical thumb imprints become the scarab's wings, or body.

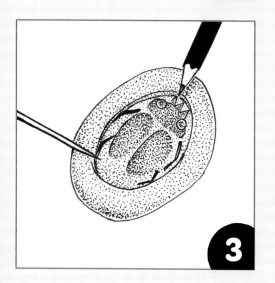

Step 3
Add other details, such as legs and eyes, by taking your toothpick and marking the modeling clay in the appropriate areas. Diagonal 1/2-inch lines near the bottom open edge of the oval shape make good beetle legs.

Step 4

Once you are satisfied with your design, begin mixing the plaster by following the package directions. It is easier if you mix it in a heavy-duty plastic bag that you can seal and then shake.

Step 5

After it is fully mixed, pour the plaster carefully into the scarab mold until it reaches the brim of the modeling clay. Allow the plaster to fully dry on a flat surface.

Step 6

Once the plaster has dried, scrape the modeling clay away from your scarab. Paint all the sides, including the bottom, with blue craft paint. When the paint has dried, add details with gold paint. After the bottom has dried completely, you can carve hieroglyphs into its surface with the end of a toothpick.

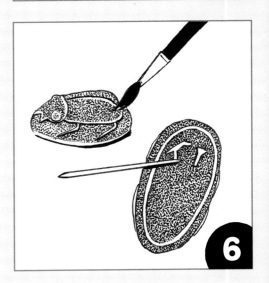

Death and the Afterlife

While ancient Egypt was not the only civilization to mummify its dead, it remains the one that is most associated with the practice. Perhaps this is because the rituals surrounding the process in Egypt were so elaborate.

The first Egyptian mummies were preserved naturally, and by accident, in dry desert sands, which acted as a preservative. However, by 3100 BC, during the First Dynasty, simple mastaba tombs were erected to house the dead. It was during this time that the process of mummification became more complex. Because the Egyptians could not immediately recreate what the dry desert sands had done naturally, they spent years experimenting with the process of preserving a body until it was perfected during the New Kingdom years. Much of what we now understand about mummification dates from this period and from studying the bodies of mummies that have been found.

Mummification was meant to purify the body of the deceased. The Egyptians considered the process a

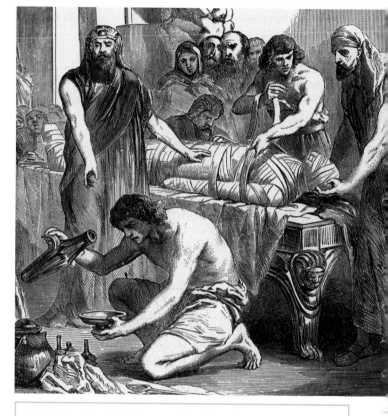

This body is being embalmed and mummified. Before being wrapped, the body cavity is stuffed with fragrant powders. After wrapping, the mummy is placed in a wooden case shaped like a human body.

religious one that would allow the body to remain recognizable to the person's *ka*, or spirit, in the afterlife. The ritual took place in a temple set aside for the purpose of embalming (preserving). The embalming temple was called the *wabet* (pure place) or *per nefer* (beautiful house) and served as a reminder that the act of preserving the body was an attempt to make it eternal and godlike.

Not only human bodies were mummified; the Egyptians often mummified their beloved pets as well. Many tombs have been found that housed animal remains. These were mostly cats and dogs, but sometimes birds, monkeys, fish, and ducks were mummified, too, and brought to special cemeteries where they were placed as offerings to the gods. In other cases, pet owners may have wanted to keep their pets with them in the afterlife, so the mummified remains were placed near the owners at the time of their own deaths. Sometimes animals were bred in captivity and sold to worshipers who had them embalmed and mummified before placing them in tombs with human remains.

Certain mummified animals were also associated with gods. Cats, for example, were linked to the cat-headed goddess, Bastet, who was said to ensure joy and motherly protection. For years, Egyptians were inspired to bring cat mummies as offerings to Bastet in the famous cat cemetery in the city of Bubastis. Many Egyptians still revere Bastet and celebrate her feast day on October 31.

Cats in ancient Egypt were admired for their grace, strength, and agility. Bronze images of cats were often placed in temples and buried in temple grounds.

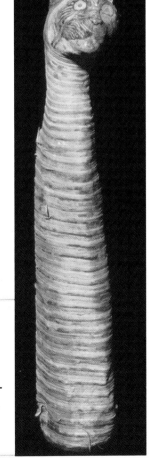

A cat mummy of the kind often offered to Bastet, the cat-headed goddess of joy and protection.

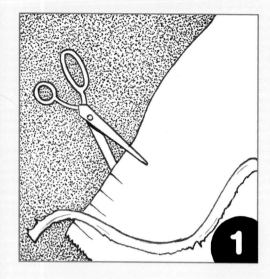

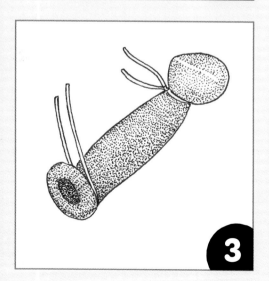

Mummified Cat

The Egyptians were the first civilization to keep cats as pets and to mummify them after death. You can perform a similar mummification ceremony by creating this cat mummy doll.

YOU WILL NEED
- Pair of tube socks
- Ten plastic bags
- Five tea bags
- Large bowl
- Needle and thread
- String
- White bed sheet or pillowcase
- Craft paint
- Small flat rocks or sea glass
- Felt-tip pen

Step 1
Take a white bed sheet and make a small cut about 1/2-inch from the bottom edge. Tear the sheet with your hands, starting from the initial cut, into a ribbonlike strip. Continue ripping lengths until you have made about twenty "bandage strips."

Step 2
Take the strips and an old pair of tube socks and put them in a bowl filled with hot tap water and five tea bags. Allow them to sit for several hours (tea will stain the fabric, giving it an antiquated appearance). Remove the strips and socks from the tea water and ring them out. Allow them to dry fully.

Step 3
Once your sock has completely dried, roll the open end into a doughnut-shape (the animal's feet). Stuff the toe of the sock with three plastic grocery bags, making a firm ball. This will be your cat mummy's

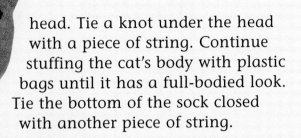

head. Tie a knot under the head with a piece of string. Continue stuffing the cat's body with plastic bags until it has a full-bodied look. Tie the bottom of the sock closed with another piece of string.

Step 4
Add ears to your animal by cutting two triangular pieces of your other sock and sewing them with a needle and thread. Paint facial features on the animal's face with black craft paint, or draw them with a black marker.

Step 5
Begin wrapping your mummy by taking a strip and tying it around the neck of your sock-animal. Wrap the width of the animal until you reach the foot area. Knot the strips together as you wind, forming one continuous strip. Wrap tightly around the feet until they are completely covered in "bandages." Having bundled the width of the cat, now begin wrapping its length by wrapping lengthwise around the neck and back down to the feet. Repeat the horizontal and vertical wrapping for an interesting layered effect.

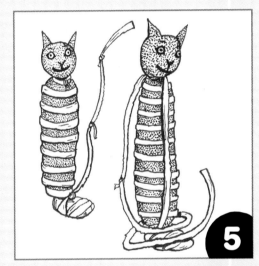

Step 6
Make amulets for your cat mummy by drawing or painting hieroglyphs on small rocks or sea glass. Hide them under the wrapped bandages to protect your mummy during its passage to the afterlife.

Mummification

The process of mummification was presided over by several priests, as well as one priest supervisor who wore the frightening mask of Anubis, the Egyptian god of the dead. It was a long religious ritual that involved the constant recitation of prayers and could last as long as seventy days.

Before the body could be wrapped, it had to be dehydrated. The body's internal organs (lungs, intestines, stomach, liver) were removed (except for the heart, which was thought to be the center of the soul) and placed in four separate canopic jars (special vessels used only for the storage of organs during mummification). During the New Kingdom period, the brain would also be removed through the nostrils. Each container represented one of the four sons of Horus (the Egyptian sky god): Imsety (represented on a jar by a human), Hapy (baboon), Duamutef (dog), and Qebehsenuef (falcon). Each of these figures was responsible for the care of the body part which it held.

This mummy was found in a tomb near Cairo. Its arms are crossed in a typical Egyptian pose known as the Osiris position.

After the internal organs were removed, the body was washed with wine and filled with dry materials such as sawdust, leaves, grasses, fabric, and incense (which kept odors at bay). Next, it was covered with a mixture of salt crystals called natron and left to dry for a period of forty days. The now-dried body would be carried to the Nile River where it would be washed. Sacred and fragrant oils would be rubbed into the mummified remains before it was carefully wrapped in as many as twenty layers of fine linen. Then the arms of the deceased would be crossed over the heart. This was known as the Osiris position. Some of the wrappings were complex and braided, and many held small charms or amulets between their folds. These amulets were thought to protect the body of the deceased while it made its journey to the afterlife and often depicted popular gods of the day or symbols such as the ankh—a looped cross that the Egyptians believed represented the "breath of life."

Not every mummification process was as elaborate as this, however. Only wealthy individuals could afford such a ritual. Throughout the centuries, most Egyptians' bodies were mummified the old-fashioned way and left to dry naturally in the desert sands.

The ankh, the Egyptian symbol of life, could be worn only by nobility, and was often inscribed on the walls of royal tombs.

Tutankhamen was a boy pharaoh who died around 1346 BC. His tomb was discovered in 1922 and contained hundreds of well-preserved artifacts.

Canopic jars with cynocephalous head, jackal's head, man's head, and falcon's head. All date from 1080 BC to 720 BC.

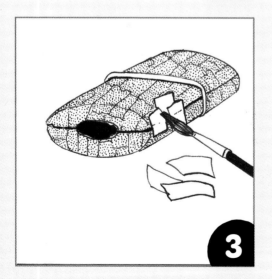

Canopic Jars*

While your canopic jars will never hold internal organs, they are just as mysterious looking as the set discovered by Jean-Francois Champollion, the French Egyptologist.

* ADULT SUPERVISION IS REQUIRED FOR THIS CRAFT.

YOU WILL NEED
- **White glue and water solution (three parts glue to one part water)**
- **Newspaper strips**
- **Small, empty liquid soap bottle**
- **Air-hardening clay**
- **Toothpicks**
- **Craft knife**
- **Scissors**
- **Craft paint**
- **Rubber bands**
- **Sponge**

Step 1
Cover an empty, small-sized, plastic liquid soap bottle with six to eight layers of papier-mâché (created by soaking newspaper strips in watered-down white glue and pasting them to the surface of the bottle). Cover the entire bottle with newspaper strips, except for the neck, allowing drying time after each layer is applied. Turn the bottle upside down to dry.

Step 2
Once the last layer of papier-mâché has fully dried, use a craft knife to cut a continuous line starting at the right side of your paper bottle (near the neck), cutting down and around the bottom, and up to the top of the opposite (left) side. Gently pull the two halves away from the plastic bottle.

Step 3
Secure the two paper "jar" halves together with a rubber band. Then, apply three additional layers of papier-mâché to reseal the jars, making the two pieces one again. Coat the entire jar, with the exception of the area covered by the rubber band. Once the rest of the jar is coated, remove the rubber band and coat that section, too. Allow jar to dry overnight.

Step 4

To make the animal-head lid, roll an egg-sized amount of clay into a ball. Press it on top of the plastic bottle you used as a mold. Shape the clay into a pyramid with a flattened top. Next, remove the clay from the plastic bottle. Set aside.

Step 5

Form a small amount of clay in a closed ring shape that is the same size as the opening of the soap bottle. Place the ring shape on the bottom of your animal-head lid and join them together using a toothpick. Test the fit of your lid by attaching it to your paper jar. Add faces to your lid, using small rolled balls of clay and simple shapes. Allow to fully dry.

Step 6

When your animal-head lid has dried, paint it with bright colors. Paint the paper jar a solid color. Once this base color has dried, add a darker color to a household sponge, and lightly dab the surface of the jar. Add other details, such as hieroglyphs, with a black or brown marker.

Lives of the Pharaohs

The pharaoh was the most powerful person in Egypt. Not only was he worshiped in much the same way that gods were worshiped, he also owned all of Egypt's land and its people. In his duties as Egypt's ruler, he had to ensure that the land remained prosperous and that the people were fed. In some cases, as in the reign of Queen Hatshepsut, women fulfilled the role of pharaoh, but this was a rare instance. As a royal wife, however, a queen would also be revered as a goddess by all of Egypt.

To keep the royal bloodline pure, a pharaoh had to produce an heir to his throne by fathering a son. In this way, an Egyptian dynasty could continue within the same family for centuries. Most pharaohs had many wives and children to ensure that there would be a rightful heir to the throne. These women all lived together in a harem—a private apartment within the palace set aside for them—and washed and dressed the pharaoh many times per day, constantly catering to his every need.

This statue adorns the temple of Hathor, part of Queen Hatshepsut's burial complex in Luxor, Egypt. Hatshepsut was the first female pharaoh of Egypt, but as was the custom, she was portrayed as a man.

Many of the pharaoh's duties were assigned to his royal court and undertaken by courtiers, high officials, high priests, and royal scribes. These individuals would live near the pharaoh or in the royal palace, each in separate quarters. They were also expected to help the royal family prepare for public appearances, which meant participation in numerous daily and very personal rituals.

This wooden box of toiletries hails from the Eighteenth Dynasty. The Egyptians commonly used scented oils as perfume and colored powders as makeup.

Each morning the pharaoh would recline in a tub of bathwater, joined by a procession of courtiers, including wig-makers (the majority of adult Egyptians shaved their heads, preferring to wear wigs instead of their own hair), sandal-makers, perfumers, launderers, and guardians of the royal wardrobe. After the bath, the courtiers would dress the pharaoh in fine linens and adorn him with makeup, perfumes, his official crown, and other royal accessories, such as a long bent staff, called a crook.

While in public, the pharaoh donned a royal nemes (a striped head-cloth), a ceremonial beard, and a crown called a uraeus that bore an image of two snakes, which the Egyptians believed would "spit fire" at the pharaoh's enemies. Part of the royal attire may have also included an ankh, the looped cross symbol that could be worn only by Egyptian royalty.

This gold coffin depicts the royal headdress, ceremonial beard, and snake crown worn only by pharaohs.

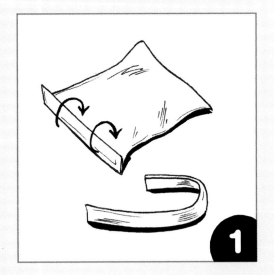

Royal Headdress

Dress like a pharaoh would by fashioning a nemes headdress and uraeus snake crown.

YOU WILL NEED

- T-shirt
- Large rubber band
- Aluminum foil
- White glue and water solution
- Newspaper strips
- String
- Scissors
- Craft paint
- Pencil
- Hole puncher

Step 1
Cut two pieces of aluminum foil, each piece 10 inches long. Take the first piece and fold a 2-inch width along the cut end. Continue folding, using this width as a guide, until one headband with a 2-inch width remains. Arch that headband around your forehead to size it properly.

Step 2
Take the second piece of foil and roll it into a slender tube. This is the snake. Hold the tube vertically, and fold it in half so that the top and bottom edges meet. Insert the headband through the single fold of the snake. Squeeze the ends of the folded tube together and bend the front down in the shape of a snake's head. If you would like your crown to have two snakes, make the second one in the same manner.

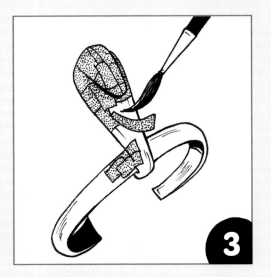

Step 3
Completely cover the headband and snake(s) with two to three layers of papier-mâché (see page 26). Allow it to dry overnight.

Step 4
Once your headband has fully dried, use a hole puncher to puncture each end of the band.

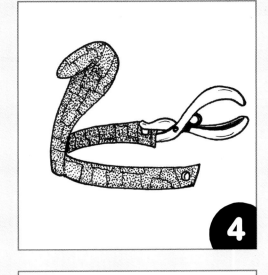

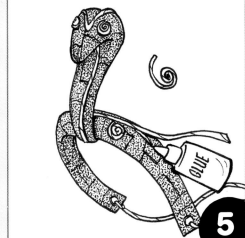

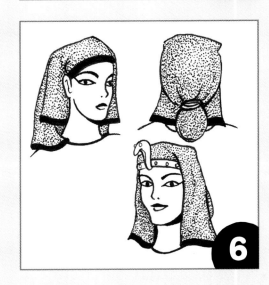

Step 5

Draw pencil designs on your headband, and then trace the designs in small sections with white glue. Place the string into the glue, holding it in place until it is secure. To make snake eyes, coil string tightly between your thumb and index finger. Drop a dab of glue onto the coil, and apply it to the head of your snake. Make outlines with glued string, and add spiraled pieces, as shown. Once the glue has dried, paint the entire headband with metallic gold paint. Knot strings to both holes.

Step 6

To make the nemes: Turn your T-shirt inside out and put it on as you would normally. Now, remove it, just enough so that its neckband remains on your forehead. Push the neckband above your ears, exposing them. Take both sleeves and let them fall past each side of your face. With a rubber band, fasten the back into a large ponytail. Place headband around your forehead. Secure it to your head by tying the two strings together.

Jewelry and the Decorative Arts

When designing their decorative arts (including painting, jewelry, furniture, clothing, and pottery), the Egyptians looked to nature for their inspiration, as demonstrated by images reproduced again and again, such as the lotus flower. Viewed as a symbol of rebirth, the lotus became a basic design for Egyptian artisans, appearing on jewelry, floor tiles, pottery, and as a hieroglyph. Most Egyptian art was sacred (inspired by religion or having a religious purpose) and completed as a service to the pharaoh. Almost all art was made anonymously.

What remains of Egyptian wall painting—such as those within homes, temples, and the tombs of the pharaohs—tells historians that it was common for artists to record daily events, mythological stories, and incidents from Egypt's historical past. These images were drawn in a similar style (colorful, flat images viewed in profile and stretching in horizontal bands across a wall) for thousands

The lotus, a symbol of rebirth, is prominently displayed during a banquet of offerings, as in this image taken from the Book of the Dead.

of years, using the same technique. First, the walls would be plastered. Then, the plastered surface was divided into a series of squares, or a grid. A drawing was applied in black or brown outlines and filled in later by a different painter.

Another typical Egyptian decorative art was jewelry. Commonly worn by all Egyptians, no matter their class, jeweled necklaces, bracelets, and rings often marked specific turning points in a person's life. Some jewelry was worn as a charm in the belief that it would keep the wearer safe; for instance, small children wore tiny fish charms in their hair while swimming in the Nile River to prevent death by drowning.

The earliest examples of Egyptian jewelry incorporated gold and semiprecious stones, such as feldspar and amethyst. Gold was also closely associated with Ra, the sun god, and its widespread use was a kind of worship of this deity. Gold was plentiful because of the many mines between the Nile River and the Red Sea. The Egyptians used it for many artistic purposes. Surviving artifacts reveal that gold was melted and molded, sometimes over wooden shapes such as royal coffins. Gold was also used to decorate the royal family's furniture. Later, traders introduced glass to the Egyptians, who held it in high regard, almost as if it were a valuable and precious gemstone.

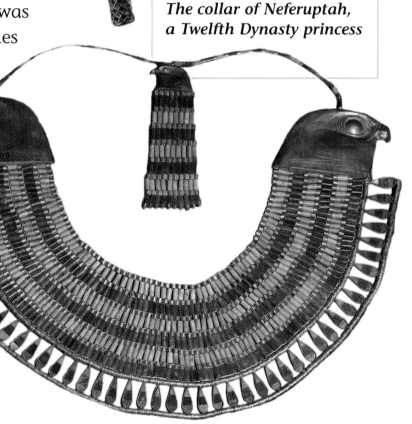

The lotus flower was an important image in Egyptian jewelry, pottery, and hieroglyphs.

Pharaohs were cooled in the hot desert sun by servants who waved fans like this one.

The collar of Neferuptah, a Twelfth Dynasty princess

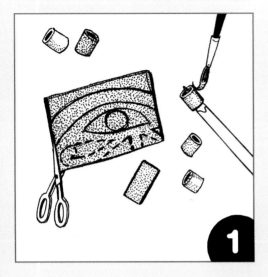

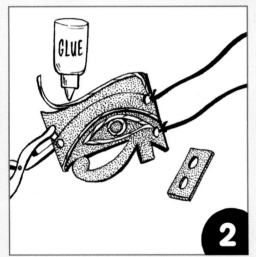

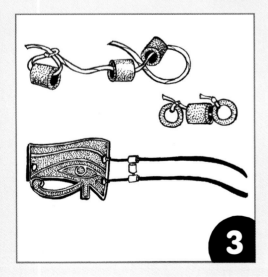

Egyptian Bracelet and Necklace

Make Egyptian bead jewelry similar in style to the designs worn by Cleopatra.

YOU WILL NEED
- Pasta noodles
- String
- Scissors
- Cardboard
- Ruler
- Pen or pencil
- Hole puncher
- Craft paint
- White glue

Step 1
Paint approximately 15–20 small pasta beads in assorted colors. Cut a piece of cardboard into a square, large enough to fit around your wrist. Also, cut a smaller cardboard rectangle for the clasp. Draw an Egyptian wadjet eye (a symbol of health and prosperity) on the cardboard square. Use the wadjet eye on page 35 as a model.

Step 2
Punch two holes on the right side of the square cardboard piece, and one on the left, as shown. In addition, punch two holes into the rectangular piece. Paint them both and add decorative detail with glued string. Tie two pieces of string, each approximately 10 inches long, to the holes on the right side of the cardboard square.

Step 3
Take a new piece of string, thread one pasta bead, and tie it securely in a knot. Next, thread two more beads. You will notice that the two added beads are

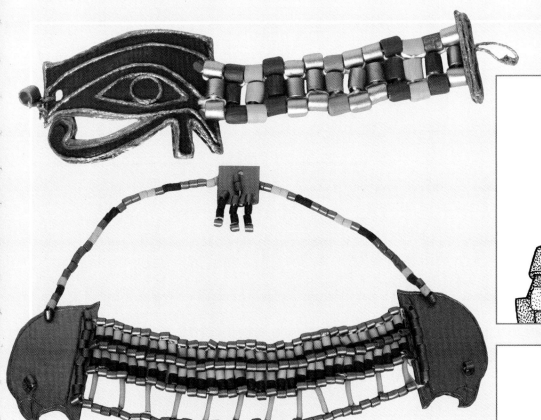

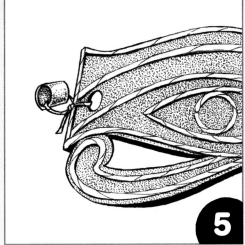

facing a different direction than the first. Loop your string between the second and third bead and tie a knot. Cut and remove the excess string. This is your first row of three beads. Thread the knotted beads through the two strings on the cardboard.

Step 4
Continue Step 3 until you have enough beads to make a bracelet suitable for your wrist size. Once you are finished, tie the small cardboard clasp to the end of your strings and knot it with a loop.

Step 5
Tie a single bead to the hole on the left side of the cardboard. To wear the bracelet, wrap the loop at the end of the bracelet around the bead.

Step 6
If you enjoyed this project, try making a necklace using longer beads and two cardboard shapes to hold the rows of strung beads together.

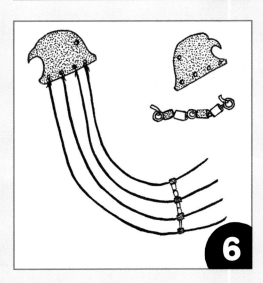

Egyptians at Home

Most Egyptian homes were decorated with frescoes—ancient paintings done on wet plaster. The Egyptians, like many other civilizations after them, used fresco painting as a way to enrich their personal space, detailing events from their lives or the lives of the pharaohs whom they served. Other artifacts show that they used ornate tiles in their homes, many depicting symbols from nature, such as lotus blossoms, in repeating patterns.

The homes of the lower classes and those of the slaves were very basic structures made entirely of mud brick and containing few if any decorative elements. Instead of tiles, floors were often painted in bright colors or just made of sand. Some Egyptians still live in traditional mud brick dwellings today, many of which have been built on the ruins of their ancestors. As in the vanished cities of the past, many of these houses are situated very close together within a maze-like series of pathways and alleys. All Egyptian homes shared one common

This Eighteenth Dynasty wooden footstool with a woven seat, straw whisk, and basket lid were found in the tomb of the royal architectural foreman Kha.

element: Every structure had a flat roof suitable for sleeping under the stars during the hottest months of the year.

Most homes, whether occupied by nobility or commoners, were sparsely furnished. Only the pharaohs and those serving them enjoyed the comforts of platform beds and chairs. Tables were found only in the wealthiest of households. Instead of wooden furniture, poor Egyptian families made household items from the dried leaves of palm trees. Other items were woven from these same leaves, such as baskets for storing grain, mats for sleeping, and stools for sitting.

This Egyptian predynastic vase is painted with a simple line drawing.

Egyptians, whether rich or poor, enjoyed using cosmetics to enhance their physical beauty. As a result, cosmetic and perfume vessels and small pots and dishes made of faience (a glazed earthenware that first appeared in 2300 BC) could be found in many Egyptian homes. Terra-cotta pottery was also very common, and Egyptian craftspeople made many vessels using ancient potter's wheels that were operated by hand; they look like the devices used today for the same purpose.

This is the chair of Queen Hetepheres. Only royalty enjoyed the comfort of chairs; poor Egyptians made do with stools woven with palm leaves.

This large bowl in blue faience is decorated with lotuses growing in a square pool.

Faience Plate

The Egyptians made many of their everyday items out of faience, a blue glazed earthenware. Practice the art of the ancient potters and create this imitation faience plate.

YOU WILL NEED
- Food coloring
- Rubber gloves
- Paintbrush
- Craft paint
- Acrylic gloss varnish
- Salt Clay

Salt Clay Recipe
2 cups salt
1 cup cornstarch
1 cup water

Mix the salt and cornstarch in a saucepan. Add water and stir completely. Heat over a low flame for about five minutes, stirring constantly. Remove the clay from the saucepan and place it on a cookie sheet to cool before modeling.

Step 1
Before you color your clay, cover your hands with rubber gloves. Add blue and green food coloring to your clay as it cools, kneading with your hands as you mix it. Make the clay dark in color; it will lighten once it dries.

Step 2
Roll the clay into a smooth ball. Flatten it on your work surface with the palm of your hand. Smooth the sides flat.

Step 3
Build up the plate's rim by lightly pinching around it. Wet your fingers and smooth the surface of your clay.

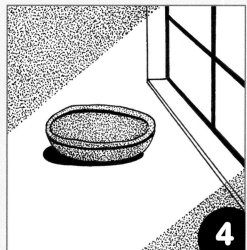

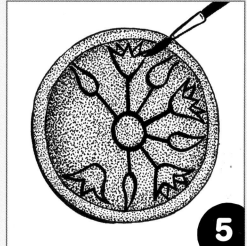

Step 4
Once the plate has been shaped, allow it to dry in a sunny window for several days. Once completely dry, it will be very hard and ready to paint.

Step 5
Design the inside of your plate with lotus blossoms using a medium-sized paintbrush and black paint.

Step 6
When it dries, coat the entire plate or bowl with acrylic gloss varnish. This will make it shiny and protect it from cracking.

Leisure and Play

Egyptians encouraged leisure activities of all sorts during the height of the Old Kingdom, when many games were invented (probably because of the increasingly easy life that new irrigation technology provided). Egyptian children played with objects we would still find familiar today, such as dolls, balls, and pull toys.

A board game called *mehen* (meaning "coiled one") was also very popular with children. It was played on a spiral board that often bore the shape and likeness of a snake. The object of this game was to begin at the tip of the snake's tail and move game balls toward its center eye. This game is also sometimes referred to as the snake game. Adults commonly played a board game called *senet* that represented a struggle between good and evil forces. The thirty squares on the board each represented a different

This is a fresco painting of Nefertari, one of Rameses II's queens, playing the game called senet.

virtue or conflict. Two players threw numbered sticks in the air to decide how to move about the board (similar to the way dice are used). Senet was popular with all classes, and many representations of the ancient game, from the simplest to the most exquisite, exist to this day.

Other leisurely pastimes included storytelling, dancing, and music. Archaeologists have unearthed beautiful harps—usually played by nobility and court musicians—crafted in the shapes of pharaohs and women. Singers also performed to the beat of drums, cymbals, bells, and rattles called sistrums. Sistrums were commonly used during religious ceremonies, too, and were carried by priests and nobility.

Dancing was popular during times of celebration or festivity. Sometimes professional dancers and musicians were called upon to entertain party guests or perform during rituals. These hired dancers were depicted in Egyptian wall paintings in acrobatic positions, such as somersaults and cartwheels.

Egyptians of all ages enjoyed playing outdoors. They swam, rode donkeys, hunted, fished for pleasure, and held tournaments for activities such as wrestling and sword fighting. Boxing and fencing were enjoyed by adult men. Most of the information we possess about how the Egyptians spent their hours of leisure was learned from reading hieroglyphs or studying images depicted on wall paintings.

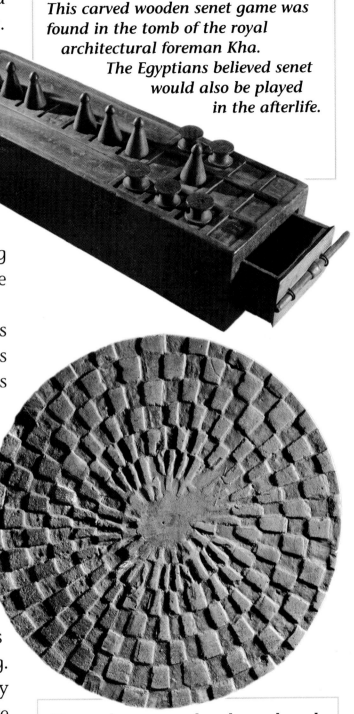

This carved wooden senet game was found in the tomb of the royal architectural foreman Kha.
The Egyptians believed senet would also be played in the afterlife.

The snake game—played on a board decorated with a spiral pattern—allowed players to move marbles and lion-shaped pieces from the serpent's tail toward its center eye.

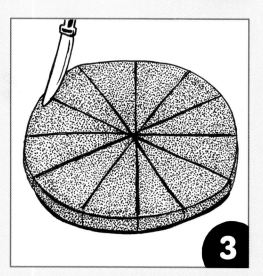

Snake Game

Copy the exact design of mehen, the Egyptians' earliest board game. The coiled design represents the snake's body, with its eye as the center. Create your own rules of play to advance the pieces from the board's outer edge to its center.

YOU WILL NEED
- Sand clay (see recipe on page 14)
- Large bowl
- Aluminum foil
- Medium frying pan
- Nonserrated knife

Step 1
Make the sand clay using the recipe on page 14. Once your clay is cool, empty it into a medium-sized frying pan. Spread it evenly.

Step 2
After your clay is shaped to the inside of the pan, allow it to sit for several minutes. Then flip the shaped clay out of the pan and onto your work surface.

Step 3
Lightly trace six lines on the surface of the clay with a knife, as if you were cutting a pizza. Do not cut through the clay to the bottom; these slices are only to mark your design. Next, draw a circle with your knife at the center of your slices. Use the top of a drinking glass if you need a pattern.

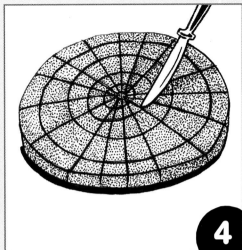

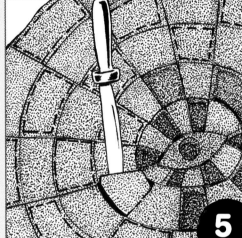

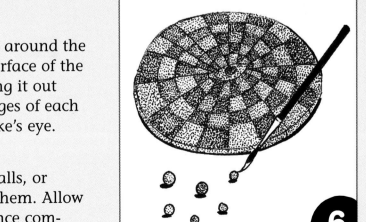

Step 4

Press your finger into the center of the clay circle. Use your knife to draw concentric rings spreading out from the center to the board's rim, as on a dartboard. Lightly slice the surface from the center to the edge without cutting the surface deeply, as shown.

Step 5

Cut alternate rectangles from the first ring around the center, like a checkerboard. Remove the surface of the clay from each alternate rectangle by lifting it out with your knife. Smooth and shape the edges of each cut. Decorate the center to resemble a snake's eye.

Step 6

Roll the removed clay into several small balls, or game pieces. Use a little water to smooth them. Allow the game board and pieces to dry fully. Once completely dry, paint them as desired.

TIMELINE

BC

3500	Egyptians begin to mummify bodies by wrapping them in strips of cloth.
3200	Egyptians develop first hieroglyphs.
3100	Sumerians invent a system of writing.
3000	Upper and Lower Egypt are united, beginning the Early Dynastic Period.
2630	Egyptians build step pyramid for King Djoser.
2613	Great Pyramids and the Sphinx in Giza are started.
2575	Egypt's Old Kingdom begins.
2360	Mesopotamian city-states unite under one king.
2040	Egypt's Middle Kingdom begins.
1985	Trade begins with Asia and the Aegean.
1730	Hyksos invades Egypt and the Israelites settle there.
1650	Mycenaean culture develops in Greece.
1580	Spells later known as the Book of the Dead first appear on the coffin of Queen Mentuhotep.
1540	New Kingdom begins in Egypt.
1350	Akhenaton and Nefertiti rule over Egypt.
1333	Tutankhamen rules over Egypt and brings back the worship of many gods.
1320	First papyrus book is made.
1304	King Ramses II rules over Egypt.
1270	Israelites leave Egypt.
1186	The Royal Tombs in the Valley of the Kings begin to be plundered.
1163	King Ramses III, the last great pharaoh of Egypt, dies.
1085	New Kingdom ends. Attackers seize area and divide it in two. Egypt loses power.
525	Egypt is invaded and captured by the Persians.
332	Alexander the Great conquers Egypt and becomes pharaoh.
31	Cleopatra and Mark Antony are defeated by the Roman emperor Octavian. Egypt falls under Roman rule.

GLOSSARY

amulet Small charm or other sacred object inserted into the wrappings of a mummy or worn for protection.

Anubis God of the dead, of mummification, and embalming.

Book of the Dead Collection of more than 200 spells that was placed with a mummy to help the deceased reach the afterlife.

canopic jars Four containers, each featuring the head of a different god, that were used to hold the internal organs of the deceased.

demotic Egyptian cursive writing that predates hieroglyphs.

Dynastic Period Time period when Egypt was governed by related pharaohs.

hieroglyph From the Greek for "sacred carving," a character used in ancient Egyptian writing.

Lower Egypt Northern part of Egypt around the Nile Delta.

Middle Kingdom Era in Egyptian history covering the years 2040–1640 BC (Eleventh to Thirteenth Dynasties).

mummy Egyptian body that has been preserved through a drying method.

New Kingdom Era in Egyptian history covering the years 1540–1070 BC (Eighteenth to Twenty-first Dynasties).

Old Kingdom Era in Egyptian history covering the years 2575–2150 BC (Third through Eighth Dynasties).

papyrus Water plant that was used to make paper.

pharaoh Ruler of Egypt who was worshiped as a god and owned all of Egypt's land and people.

Ra Egyptian sun god who took many different forms.

reservoir Body of water reserved for farming or other public use.

Rosetta Stone Three-foot-high stone monument dating back to 196 BC, in which three different languages—hieroglyph, demotic, and Greek—represent the same text; a message of thanks to Pharaoh Ptolemy V.

scarab Egyptian dung beetle sculpture, usually carved with hieroglyphs on its underside; a symbol of rebirth.

Upper Egypt Southern part of the country extending along the Nile from Memphis to the cataracts, a stretch of river rapids.

Valley of the Kings Valley on the west bank of the Nile River near Luxor, which contains the tombs of many pharaohs.

FOR MORE INFORMATION

ORGANIZATIONS

The Archaeological Institute of America
Boston University
656 Beacon Street
Boston, MA 02215-2006
Web site: http://www.archaeology.org

Metropolitan Museum of Art
1000 Fifth Avenue
New York, NY 10028
(212) 535-7710
Web site: http://www.metmuseum.org

Smithsonian Institution Information Center
1000 Jefferson Drive SW
Washington, DC 20560-0010
(202) 357-2700
Web site: http://www.si.edu

University of Pennsylvania Museum of Archaeology and Anthropology
33rd and Spruce Streets
Philadelphia, PA 19104
(215) 898-4001
Web site: http://www.upenn.edu/museum

World Archaeological Society
120 Lakewood Drive
Hollister, MO 65672
(417) 334-2377

In Canada

Royal Ontario Museum
100 Queen's Park
Toronto, ON M5S 2C6
(416) 586-8000
Web site: http://www.rom.on.ca

WEB SITES

Dig! the Archaeology Magazine for Kids
http://www.digonsite.com

Pyramids: The Inside Story
http://www.pbs.org/wgbh/nova/pyramid

Tutankhamen
http://www.nationalgeographic.com/egypt

FOR FURTHER READING

Champan, Gillian. *The Egyptians (Crafts From the Past)*. San Diego, CA: Heinemann Publishers, 1997.

Hart, George. *Eyewitness: Ancient Egypt*. New York: DK Publishing, 2000.

Shuter, Jane. *Ancient Egypt: History Beneath Your Feet*. New York: Raintree/Steck-Vaughn, 2000.

Smith, Brenda. *Egypt of the Pharaohs*. San Diego, CA: Lucent Books, 1996.

Wassynger, Ruth Akamine. *Ancient Egypt*. New York: Scholastic, 1999.

INDEX

ABOUT THE AUTHOR AND ILLUSTRATOR

Joann Jovinelly and Jason Netelkos have been working together on one project or another for more than a decade. This is their first collaborative series for young readers. They live in New York City.

PHOTO CREDITS

Cover scarab, p. 17 bottom © Brooklyn Museum of Art; other cover craft photographs by Cindy Reiman; p. 4 © Valley of the Kings, Thebes/Kurt Scholz/SuperStock; p. 5 © North Wind Picture Archives; pp. 6, 7, 29 top, 33 middle/bottom, 36, 37 middle, 40, 41 top/bottom © Gianni Dagli Orti/Corbis; pp. 8, 16, 29 bottom, 32, 37 top © Archivo Iconografico, S.A./Corbis; p. 9 © Vallee des Nobles-Tombe de Sennedjem, Thebes/Giraudon, Paris/SuperStock; pp. 11, 25 middle, 28 © SuperStock; p. 12 © Roger Wood/Corbis; p. 13 top © Charles & Josette Lenars/Corbis, bottom © SuperStock; p. 17 top © Martin Rogers/Corbis; pp. 20, 24 © Bettmann/Corbis; p. 21 top © Christie's Images/SuperStock, bottom © Brooklyn Museum of Art; p. 25 bottom © Founders Society Purchase, Bernard and Theresa Shulman Foundation Fund, photograph © The Detroit Institute of Arts; p. 33 top © Nik Wheeler/Corbis; p. 37 bottom © Brooklyn Museum of Art; all craft illustrations and crafts by Jason Netelkos; all craft photographs by Cindy Reiman.

SERIES DESIGN AND LAYOUT

Evelyn Horovicz